Be a Virus Warrior!

A Kid's Guide to Keeping Safe

Eloise Macgregor

PowerKiDS press

Many thanks to Matthew Winawer for being our first reader!

Published in 2020 by The Rosen Publishing Group, Inc.
29 East 21st Street, New York, NY 10010

Produced for The Rosen Publishing Group, Inc. by Alix Wood Books
Written by Eloise Macgregor
Designed and illustrated by Alix Wood

Names: Macgregor, Eloise.
Title: Be a virus warrior! a kid's guide to keeping safe / Eloise Macgregor.
Description: New York : PowerKids Press, 2020.
Identifiers: ISBN 9781725330634 (pbk.) | ISBN 9781725330641 (library bound) | ISBN 9781725330658 (ebook)
Subjects: LCSH: Viruses--Juvenile literature. | Virus diseases--Juvenile literature. | Communicable diseases--Juvenile literature.
Classification: LCC QR365.M32 2020 | DDC 579.2--dc23

Image credits:
All illustrations © Alix Wood

Manufactured in the United States of America

CPSIA Compliance Information: Batch #CSPK20: For Further Information contact
Rosen Publishing, New York, New York at 1-800-237-9932

Find us on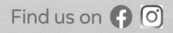

My son Matthew and I read *Be a Virus Warrior! A Kid's Guide to Keeping Safe* together. In a time when children and parents are looking for information about COVID-19, in a time of uncertainty, we found this book to be medically accurate, useful, and a good read. — Dr. Neil Winawer, Hospitalist and Professor of Medicine, Emory University School of Medicine

Contents

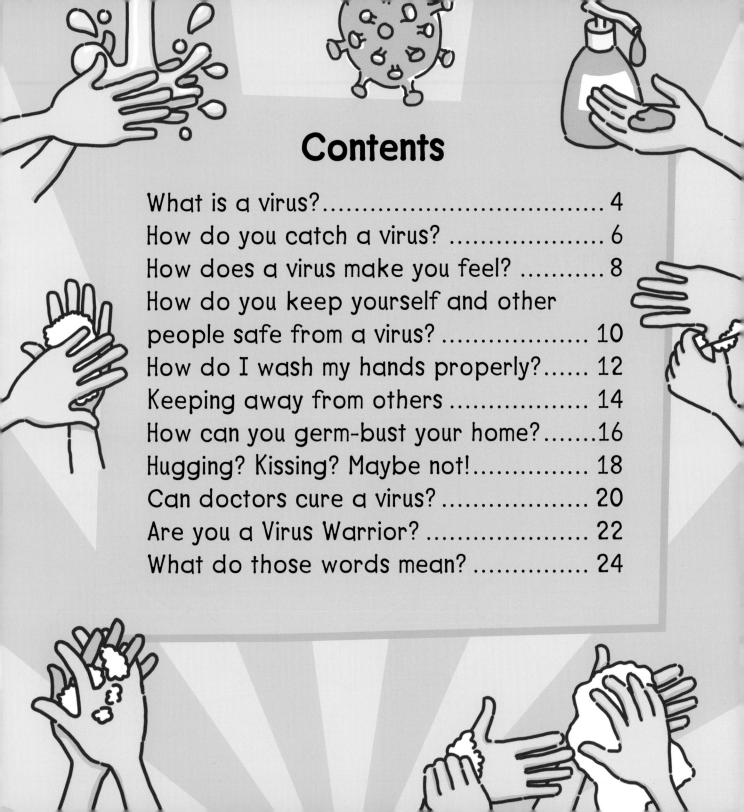

What is a virus?

A **virus** is a type of **germ**. They are very, very tiny so you can't see them. When they get inside your body, they can make you sick.

Viruses look like this, but a GAZILLION times smaller!

There are lots of different types of viruses.

There is a cold virus...

a chicken pox virus...

a flu virus…

and **coronavirus**.

People are talking a lot about coronavirus right now. Scientists have noticed a new coronavirus germ called **COVID-19**. It causes an illness a little like the flu.

How do you catch a virus?

Viruses enter your body through your nose, mouth, or eyes. Viruses can be passed from person to person. When a person coughs or sneezes, they spray the virus into the air. Another person might then breathe the virus germs in through their nose or mouth.

You might catch a virus by holding someone's hand, or giving them a kiss, or hugging them.

Germs can be left on things an ill person has touched. If you touch the same thing and then touch your face, you might catch the virus.

Try to keep a distance of about 3 to 6 feet from people with coughs or sneezes.

Wash your hands often, and don't touch your face.

How does a virus make you feel?

Different viruses can make you sick in different ways. You might get:

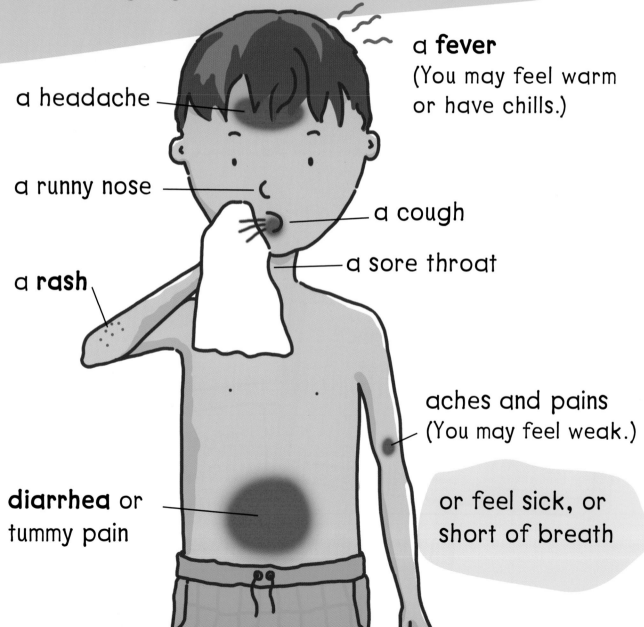

a headache

a runny nose

a **rash**

diarrhea or tummy pain

a **fever**
(You may feel warm or have chills.)

a cough

a sore throat

aches and pains
(You may feel weak.)

or feel sick, or short of breath

The **symptoms** of coronavirus are:

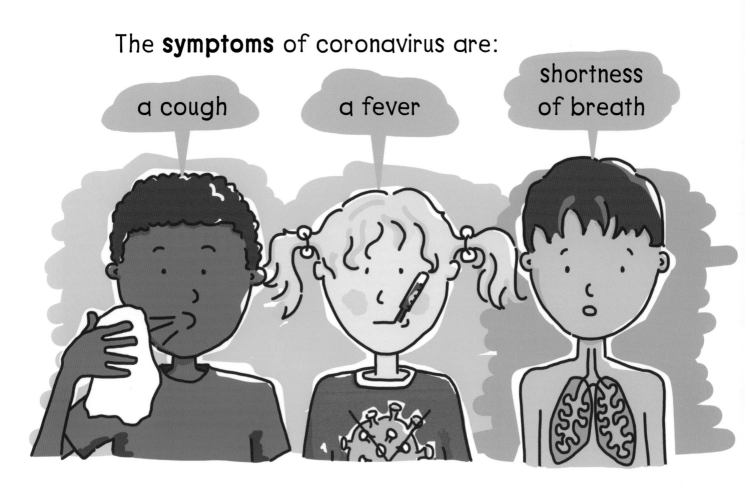

a cough

a fever

shortness of breath

Having these symptoms doesn't mean you have coronavirus. You might have a cold or the flu.

If you have been near someone with coronavirus, or been somewhere people have coronavirus, then you might have the illness.

How do you keep yourself and other people safe from a virus?

If YOU feel unwell, you need to be careful not to spread your germs.

Sneeze, cough, and blow your nose into a tissue. Then throw the tissue away.

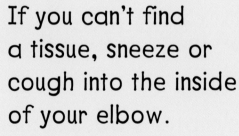

If you can't find a tissue, sneeze or cough into the inside of your elbow.

You could wear a mask if you feel unwell, to keep you from spreading your germs.

What are the best ways to make sure you don't catch a virus?

1. Wash your hands with soap. A lot!

2. Do not touch your face. Your hands may have picked up germs that can get in your nose, eyes, or mouth.

3. Try to stay away from anyone who appears unwell, or anyone who has been with people who are unwell. They may look fine, but may be **carrying** a virus.

11

How do I wash my hands properly?

Wash your hands for at least 20 seconds. That's about the same time as singing "Happy Birthday" all the way through twice. Follow the routine below.

Wet hands with water.

Use soap.

Rub your palms together.

Cross your fingers and palms. Then cross fingers, backs of hands together.

Clean the backs of your hands.

Clean your thumbs.

Clean your fingernails and the ends of your fingers.

Clean your wrists.

Rinse with water.

Dry your hands well with a clean paper towel, and throw it away.

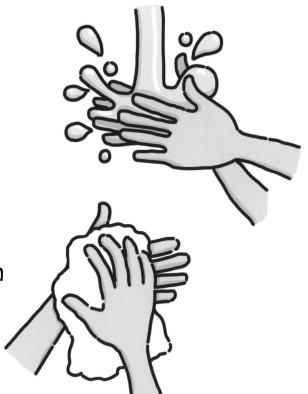

13

Keeping away from others

To stop a virus from spreading, sometimes you may be asked to keep yourself away from other people. Your school may shut, and events you wanted to go to might be canceled. You may even have to stay in your home, which doctors call **self-isolation**.

It's important to make sure you do as you are asked. Some people might get very ill if they catch a virus. Old people and people who are already ill need to be protected.

It can actually be fun to be in isolation! You can watch some movies. Play board games. Read a book. Do some coloring.

How can you germ-bust your home?

Easy! Keep your hands clean, and clean the places people touch often in your home.

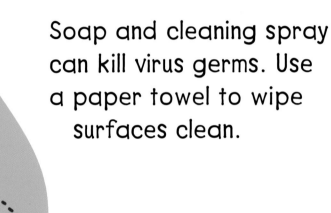

Soap and cleaning spray can kill virus germs. Use a paper towel to wipe surfaces clean.

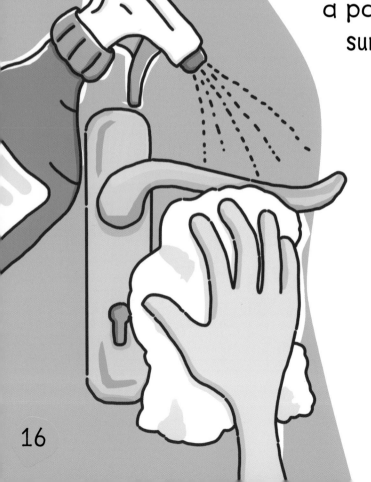

Viruses can survive a long time on surfaces. Wipe commonly used surfaces, door handles, and light switches.

Then throw away the paper towel and wash your hands.

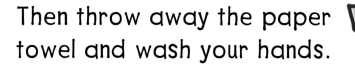

Think your family might not wash their hands as well as you? Their not-very-clean hands may have touched that faucet!

You can turn some faucets on and off using your elbows, like doctors do. Or turn them using a paper towel.

Hugging? Kissing? Maybe not!

Think you may be unwell? Or is a friend or member of your family ill? You may want to change how close you get to them for now.

Germs can get passed on easily through a handshake or a kiss. It is a good idea to not kiss and hug if someone has a virus.

You can still show
people that you care.

You can give
them a smile.

Or bump elbows!

Or make them a
"get well" card.

Get Well
Soon

Can doctors cure a virus?

You can be protected against some viruses by being given a **vaccine**. A vaccine is medicine that helps you fight a virus.

There are vaccines for chicken pox and flu. You may have had some vaccines when you were a baby.

New viruses, like the new coronavirus, do not have a vaccine yet. Doctors are working hard to make one.

What can you do if you or your family
get ill with a virus?

☑ Don't worry. Most people are only ill for
a few days.

☑ Stay at home and call the doctor.

☑ Go to bed.

☑ Open the window a little if you can.

☑ Drink plenty.

☑ Make sure you don't spread
the virus to anyone else.

Pretty soon you will be better.

Are you a Virus Warrior?

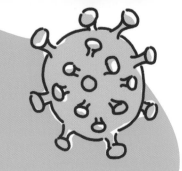

Try this quiz and see if you have the power to battle a virus! The answers are at the bottom of page 24.

1. How long should you wash your hands for?
   a) 5 seconds
   b) 10 seconds
   c) 20 seconds

2. Want to sneeze and have no tissue? What do you do?
   a) Sneeze into your inside elbow.
   b) Sneeze on some food.
   c) Sneeze on a door handle.

3. Why should you stay away from people
   if you have a virus?
   a) Old people and ill people might catch
      it and be very ill.
   b) You don't like people.

4. What can you do to help protect yourself?
   a) Wash your hands.
   b) Don't touch your face.
   c) Keep away from people with the virus.
   d) All of these answers.

Don't get too scared of viruses. Just remember – wash your hands a lot and don't touch your face. Then you probably won't catch one or spread one!

What do those words mean?

carrying not suffering from a disease, but having the infection and being able to give the disease to someone else.

coronavirus a type of virus.

COVID-19 a new illness that can affect your lungs that is caused by a virus called coronavirus.

diarrhea frequent and watery poop.

fever a rise of body temperature above the normal.

germ a microscopic living thing that causes disease.

rash a breaking out of the skin with red spots.

self-isolation the act of separating oneself from others.

symptom a physical change that indicates the presence of a disease.

vaccine a preparation given, often by injection, to keep you from getting a disease.

virus a tiny infectious agent that can grow and multiply in living cells and cause disease in plants, animals, and human beings.

Quiz answers: 1 c, 2 a, 3 a, 4 d